ENGINEERING MARVELS

BUILDING THE
CHANNEL TUNNEL

KELLY DOUDNA

Consulting Editor, Diane Craig, M.A./Reading Specialist

Super Sandcastle

An Imprint of Abdo Publishing
abdopublishing.com

abdopublishing.com

Published by Abdo Publishing, a division of ABDO, PO Box 398166, Minneapolis, Minnesota 55439. Copyright © 2018 by Abdo Consulting Group, Inc. International copyrights reserved in all countries. No part of this book may be reproduced in any form without written permission from the publisher. Super SandCastle™ is a trademark and logo of Abdo Publishing.

Printed in the United States of America, North Mankato, Minnesota
062017
092017

THIS BOOK CONTAINS
RECYCLED MATERIALS

Editor: Lauren Kukla
Content Developer: Mighty Media, Inc.
Cover and Interior Design and Production: Mighty Media, Inc.
Photo Credits: Alamy; AP Images; iStockphoto; Kecko/Flickr; Kzaral/Flickr; Mighty Media, Inc.; Shutterstock; Wikimedia Commons

Publisher's Cataloging-in-Publication Data

Names: Doudna, Kelly, author.
Title: Building the Channel Tunnel / by Kelly Doudna.
Description: Minneapolis, MN : Abdo Publishing, 2018. | Series: Engineering marvels.
Identifiers: LCCN 2016962885 | ISBN 9781532111099 (lib. bdg.) | ISBN 9781680788945 (ebook)
Subjects: LCSH: Channel Tunnel--France--Juvenile literature. | Tunnels--Design and construction--Juvenile literature. | Civil engineering--Juvenile literature.
Classification: DDC 624--dc23
LC record available at http://lccn.loc.gov/2016962885

Super SandCastle™ books are created by a team of professional educators, reading specialists, and content developers around five essential components—phonemic awareness, phonics, vocabulary, text comprehension, and fluency—to assist young readers as they develop reading skills and strategies and increase their general knowledge. All books are written, reviewed, and leveled for guided reading, early reading intervention, and Accelerated Reader™ programs for use in shared, guided, and independent reading and writing activities to support a balanced approach to literacy instruction.

CONTENTS

WHAT IS A TUNNEL?

A tunnel is a **passage**. It is dug through the earth. It can be small or large. Tunnels run underground. The Channel Tunnel is under the English Channel. It connects England and France. Trains travel through it.

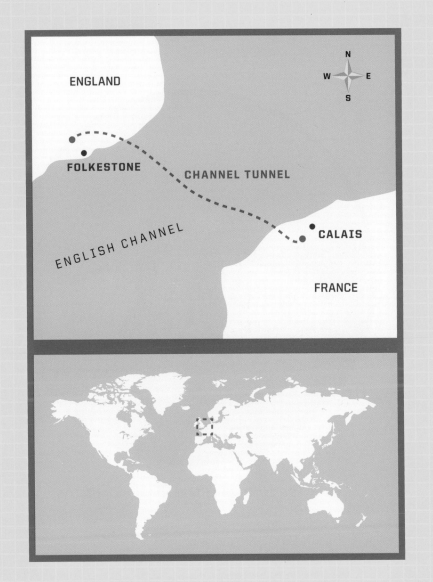

THE CHANNEL TUNNEL

LOCATION: The English Channel, Europe

ENDPOINTS: Folkestone, England, and Calais, France

BUILDING STARTED: February 2, 1988

OPENING DATE: May 6, 1994

DESIGN AND CONSTRUCTION: TransManche Link (TML)

DEEPEST POINT: 246 feet (75 m)

LENGTH: 31.4 miles (50.5 km)

NICKNAME: The Chunnel

EARLY IDEAS

It used to be hard for people to cross the English Channel. People used boats. But the water was often choppy. The trip was risky. A French engineer had an idea in the early 1800s. He wanted to build a tunnel. It would go under the channel. English leaders felt the tunnel would be unsafe. They did not support the idea.

The cliffs of Dover, England, on the English Channel

English and French companies teamed up in 1880. They dug short tunnels on each side of the channel. But the English government stopped the project.

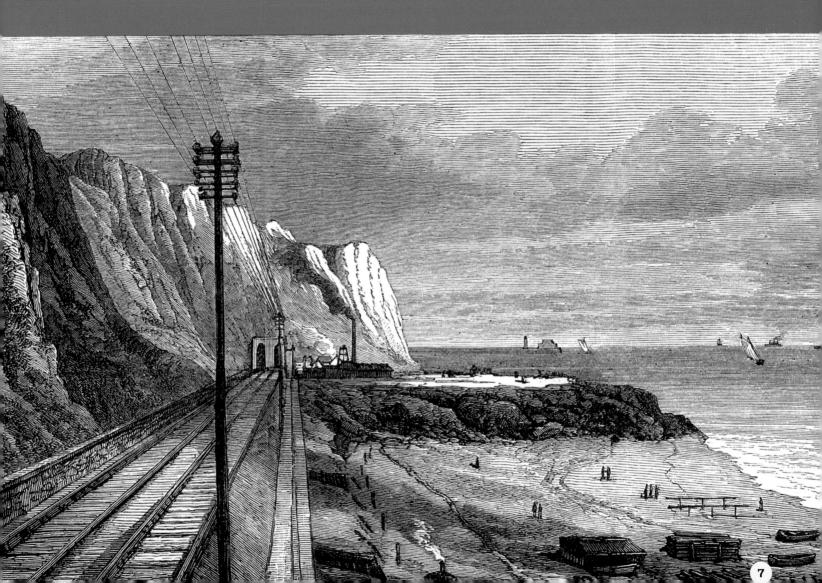

MOVING FORWARD

In the early 1900s, much of Europe was at war. English leaders felt a tunnel was risky. It would make it easier to **invade** England. So no work was done on a tunnel during this time.

By the 1980s, English and French leaders were ready for a tunnel. They agreed on a plan in 1985. The two governments signed a treaty the next year. Work began in 1988.

English troops during World War II

Engineers working on the Channel Tunnel

TRANSMANCHE LINK

No one person designed the Channel Tunnel. TransManche Link (TML) was a group of companies. They were from England and France. They joined together to build a tunnel. The group included five banks. They helped pay for the tunnel. TML also had ten construction companies. They planned and built the tunnel.

SAFETY FIRST

TML's engineers needed to make sure the tunnel was safe. There could be a fire in it. **Passengers** would need a way out. So TML planned three tunnels. Two larger tunnels were for trains. A smaller service tunnel ran between the other two. It could be an escape route.

Engineers chose a route through the English Channel. There, the sea floor was sturdy enough to hold a tunnel.

DRILLING

Digging began in 1988. Two teams dug at both ends. TML used special tunnel boring machines to dig. The front of each machine had a cutting head. The head spun around. It drilled through the rock. The new tunnel's walls were lined with concrete. This kept water from seeping in.

Rock and other material removed from the English end of the tunnel was turned into a park called Samphire Hoe.

Eleven tunnel boring machines could dig 250 feet (76.2 m) a day!

CONNECTING THE TUNNELS

TML dug the service tunnel first. In December 1990 its two parts were connected. Two people shook hands through a hole between the two sides! The other tunnels were connected in 1991. Next, workers put railroad tracks in the large tunnels. The Channel Tunnel opened on May 6, 1994.

England's Queen Elizabeth II (right) and French president François Mitterrand (center) held a celebration to open the tunnel.

TUNNEL TRAFFIC

The Channel Tunnel is a popular way to cross the English Channel. More than 50,000 people use it each day! The trip takes only 35 minutes. **Passengers** travel by train. Freight trains move **cargo**. Up to 400 trains go through the tunnel daily!

Big trains can carry cars, buses, and trucks.

TERRIFIC
TUNNEL

The Channel Tunnel is very important. It connects England with Europe. It makes it easier for people to travel between the two. More than 360 million people have used the tunnel since it opened. It is an engineering marvel. The Channel Tunnel is the eleventh-longest in the world. It has the longest underwater part of any tunnel.

Parts from one of the drills used to build the tunnel can be seen in France.

Riders board a Channel Tunnel train at Saint Pancras Station in London, England.

TUNNELS
OF THE WORLD

EISENHOWER TUNNEL

LOCATION: Colorado

BUILT: 1973

LENGTH: 1.7 miles (2.7 km)

BENEFITS: makes **transportation** easier through Colorado's Rocky Mountains

SEIKAN TUNNEL

LOCATION: Tsugaru Strait, Japan

BUILT: 1988

LENGTH: 33.5 miles (53.9 km)

BENEFITS: trains carry people and **cargo** underwater between two Japanese islands

The Channel Tunnel is just one of many awesome tunnels.
Check out these other cool tunnels!

LAERDAL TUNNEL
LOCATION: Norway

BUILT: 2000

LENGTH: 15.2 miles (24.5 km)

BENEFITS: connects the Norwegian
cities of Laerdal and Aurland, allowing
people to travel through mountains in
bad weather

GOTTHARD BASE TUNNEL
LOCATION: Swiss Alps

BUILT: 2016

LENGTH: 35.5 miles (57.1 km)

BENEFITS: trains carry people and
cargo through the mountains of
Switzerland, connecting the Swiss
towns of Erstfeld and Bodio

MORE ABOUT
THE CHANNEL TUNNEL

More than 1.5 million **DOGS AND CATS** have traveled through the Channel Tunnel.

The Channel Tunnel parts did not meet perfectly in the middle during construction. The English actually **TUNNELED FARTHER**.

The Channel Tunnel has been closed three times because of **FIRES**.

TEST YOUR KNOWLEDGE

1. The Channel Tunnel connects England and France. TRUE OR FALSE?

2. On what date did the Channel Tunnel open?

3. What kind of **vehicles** carry **passengers** through the Channel Tunnel?

THINK ABOUT IT!

Is there a tunnel near where you live? Does it go under land, or water, or other roads?

GLOSSARY

cargo – goods carried on a ship, plane, or other vehicle.

invade – to enter a place, such as a city or country, in order to take control of it.

passage – a long narrow space that connects two places.

passenger – a person riding in something, such as a car, train or bus.

transportation – the act of moving people and things.

vehicle – a machine used to carry people or goods.